Observations

Book of Poetry

Millicent Arlene Smith

BookLeaf Publishing

India | USA | UK

Made with ❤ on the BookLeaf Publishing Platform
www.bookleafpub.in
www.bookleafpub.com

Dedication

To the One, and the Only ONE!

Preface

This book of poetry comes from my observations of travel, relationships with family, friends, strangers, and being a docent at the Carnegie Museum of Art.

A Flower Growing in a Crack in the Cement

There is a flower somewhere growing through a small crack in the cement. It doesn't know it shouldn't be there. It doesn't know that most people who pass that way will never see it. It only knows it is destined to grow and be the beauty it is meant to be. It only knows that light was given so that it would grow to the best of its ability.

There is a flower somewhere, and it awaits the
opportunity to provide joy to the one who
sees it. Its only job is to BE!

And all who are given the moment to see it
will see the beauty that it is and smile
and know that GOD does exist.

3,000 Trees

There's something about to happen, and I can feel it at the very tips of my toes.
It's greater than I can ever imagine, and I'll be given a chance to be a part of it.

It's going to be HUGE!

I get to do something that cannot be explained, something that no one would have ever thought could happen to me without a reason. I won't go by fire—that can be easily explained by man.
I'll just lay down my life. I'll give it up for something greater than me.

What's the line? If a tree falls in the woods
and no one's there, does it make a sound? I'll
make a sound.
You might not hear it the moment it happens,
but it will reverberate throughout the world
for centuries to come.

I'm going to bow down to that which cannot
be explained or understood. To that which is
greater than me.

I bow down and give back my life to my
Creator.

The Garden in the Rue Cortot, Montmartre

Yeah, I hear it all the time.
"The flowers are so beautiful. There's so much
texture in the brush strokes.
It's almost like the flowers are here in the
room with us."
But I'm just as important in this painting as
the flowers are... I'M THE CONNECTOR!
What else in this painting connects the
foreground to the background?
I connect the flowers to the two guys in the
back who are goofing off. (Made you look.)

In the future, when you want to dismiss the
barren, dull brown, lifeless piece in this
painting,
remember what I do here! Without me, there
is no balance.

So, for all those things in your life you think
have no meaning, they do!
Thus ends the lesson for the day.

Soldiers' Photo

I don't know if I'm related to any of you pictured here. I found this photo in my mother's closet after her funeral. My mother didn't raise me, so I don't know if any of you are still alive. All I know is that right now, I have tears in my eyes because I can't imagine what life was like for you serving in the Armed Forces during the war. I hope all of you at least survived the war, got married, and had families of your own. I hope that in your life you were able to accomplish some of your dreams.

I don't know who you are, but I feel joy just looking at your faces, and you have touched me.

Sunrise

I sit here and watch as the sun rises for a new day of life. This big orange ball of light will provide the ability for many to see. We are given the opportunity, with this new day of light, to see what beauty is around us. We can also see what needs to be done to help make this day better than yesterday.

Every morning, when I'm able to watch the new dawn, I'm also aware of another day. I get to choose how I want to go about my day. What do I have planned for my life, and what steps do I need to take on this day to achieve my goals?

Sunrise, the dawn of a new day, another chance to observe and wonder what this day of new events and experiences will bring into my life.

Streets of Assisi, Italy

The streets wind upwards, and the path is narrow. The row houses line the path to the top, and there are many religious symbols visible to all who walk along the street. The path is clean, so no one needs to worry about stumbling on their way.

There is a connection between all the tourists and inhabitants of this town. It's quiet here. Like a sacred silence that keeps everyone in a solemn mood. There's reverence for all that is within this town. Walking the streets of Assisi becomes a place for deep thought and quiet. A walking meditation.

Sacred Space

There is a space I know of that's beautiful and kept immaculate. Not everyone is allowed to see it or spend time in this room. Only those who have been deemed worthy are permitted entry.

The reason people are kept out of this sacred space is that the one who opens the door must know those who are allowed in will revere the space and treat it gently.

There's a sacred space I know of, and it is in my heart.

Houses

I have an identical twin who stands by my side. We were built in a part of the city that became very popular due to the proximity of the colleges. We may look boring to some who pass by, but our walls have different stories to tell. Sure, we were built as a single-family home years ago, but the student population outgrew the dormitories. Now, our insides have been torn up to create new individual housing spaces.

It's okay with me. Although I no longer get to experience one family's growth, I do get to experience the vitality and excitement that student life brings to my rooms. Yes, there's banging, shouting, and partying sometimes, but I would rather experience that instead of emptiness. You know what I mean. A family grows up, the children leave home, and the parents need less space. Rooms are shut off, not used at all, and part of the house dies.

So for now, bring on the students. I'm happy knowing I'm providing a safe space for the students. A place to study, be with friends, and help create our future!

Tapestry

The colors are bold, and the textures are rich in touch and appearance. Although the colors don't seem to coordinate well with each other, when you look at the total artwork, they do. Isn't this what our lives are all about? The piecing of different cultures and races together to create beauty and harmony out of a complex combination of people.

When looking at the total world, don't we enjoy the richness that comes into our lives

where we can enjoy the other cultures and
races? Aren't our lives more harmonious when
we embrace those who might not look like
us?

Together we create a beautiful weaving—a
wonderful, rich tapestry of life that brings us
joy.

Reflections

I walked by a glass and steel building and saw a reflection of myself. I wasn't sure I really liked what I saw. Am I that heavy? When did my forehead start to become so pronounced? How was I really seen by others? I think I know how I look to others because I see myself in the mirror at home. But...it's a reflection; it's really the opposite of how others see me. In the mirror, my left ear is really my right ear. So...through my eyes, what do I really see? The opposite, or another angle? I can't see my back without using a mirror. What is the importance of seeing ourselves this way? Is it just to make sure our clothes are on correctly? And what about my inner self? Does my inner self care about what my outer body looks like? Can I be looking perfectly fit and put together but inside be so strung out that I'm about to scream?

Animals don't care what they look like. Their existence, other than cleaning themselves, is about becoming the best of their species. Does a lion care how well his mane looks when a predator comes close? But we know that in our human existence, how we look does matter to others. I think of all the times I've seen others and made a comment to myself about their appearance—how they were dressed or if their hair didn't look good. Most of those times I tried to correct myself and say something positive about what they probably had or experienced that I hadn't yet. Like, she's probably a good cook or has children who love her. We make judgments daily about what we see. I remember hearing Ray Charles on a talk show say that his blindness helped him with his relationships with others. He explained that his relationships weren't built on what people looked like but on their character. I liked that statement.

So I look at my image reflecting back to me, and yes, I do appreciate compliments on my hair, clothing, etc., but what I really hope others see is someone filled with light, hope, and love.

Crossroads

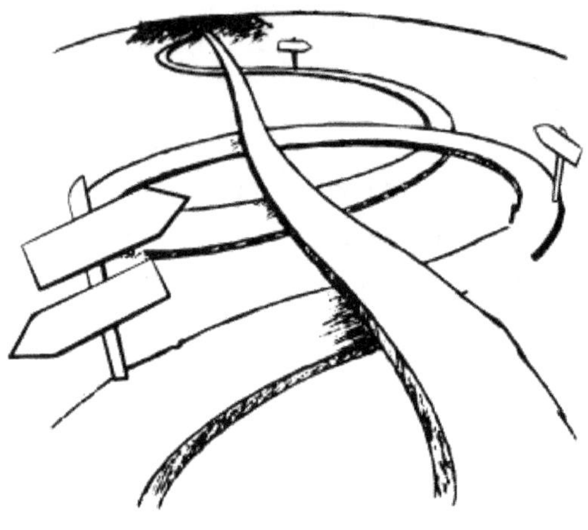

There is a point in your life where you have to face a crossroad—a point where what's on the other side of that road changes everything in your life. For me, the first major crossroad was going from living at home to getting my first apartment. I was now living on my own and making my own decisions on how to live my life. I was free! However, I did not realize how huge the feeling of being physically alone in my new home was. Yes, it was fun getting out of bed on the weekends anytime I wanted. I could leave my clothes around the room, leave unwashed dishes in the sink, or refuse to clean on certain days. But those moments of joy soon faded as I realized the most important part of my life was how I entertained myself. How was I going to occupy my mind, nourish my spirit, and enjoy my life? Who would I invite into my home? How would I spend those non-working hours? When you're young, you have friends at work to hang out with, or even family members. But as an introvert, having a lot of people in my home, in my sanctuary, was not an option. Hobbies, some sports, and other activities, such as going to the movie theaters, soon became something I planned for on my weekends.

There are crossroads of the death of a close loved one. How do I fill in the void that is left when that relationship is gone forever?

Now my new crossroad is my physical aging. There are things I can no longer do because of arthritis, stroke, allergies, and other ailments.

I now have to plan how to adjust my life to
this new reality of limitations.

There are crossroads—intersections we can
plan for—and some that come unexpectedly.
But this is life, and we adjust to each
crossroad if we intend to live it well.

Strangers

I walked by a stranger today and smiled. He said to me, "You have a beautiful smile." I thanked him, and it made me smile all the more. There is a Bible verse, Hebrews 13:2, that talks about being kind to strangers. I think back on the compliments I have received from strangers, and in those chance meetings, the compliment meant so much more than when I'm given a compliment from family or friends. Why would that be? Something has drawn the stranger to me in a way that caused them to speak to me. I hope it is because there is some light in me they see and they speak to the light.

I remember the two strangers I approached in the museum in Santa Fe, New Mexico. I saw them discussing a painting, and being a docent at an art museum, I can't stop myself from wanting to discuss art with another. The older gentleman told me that he and his nephew were visiting from North Dakota and that they were Lakota. He went on to explain the symbols in the painting that reflected their lifestyles. This chance meeting was the most cherished moment of this trip. Two strangers welcomed me to be a part of their conversation. What was it about me that made them feel comfortable talking with me and telling me about their lives?

Are these strangers I meet the angels mentioned in the Bible verse? Are these compliments and conversations a sign that the light I carry is shining brightly? I love it when I'm out and I smile at a stranger walking towards me, and they smile back. For in that moment, all is well!

Museums

I volunteer as a docent at an art museum—a position I was called to become years ago. I have always loved visiting museums when traveling to other cities since I was younger. I love seeing all of the creative expressions from artists from all over the world. My favorite Bible verse is The Master and the Talents, and I feel fortunate to volunteer in a space where I get to share the talents of many artists from all over the world with visitors who come to the museum. But it's not just the art itself that is so special to me, it's also the wonderful conversations I have with visitors who come to the museum from around the world. The joy of sharing these artworks and hearing the visitors' interpretations and how the art affects them is priceless to me.

A museum is a place where objects are displayed and preserved. Museums are also places where people from different cultures and races can come together and experience the artistic expressions and talents of artists from other cultures.

There are objects in museums that are older than most of us in age. Yet, we are able to enjoy how past generations expressed themselves through their creative skills. Museums are timeless!

Church

At my church, I'm able to not only sing and worship, but also get to be with my family, who are believers like me. It's a beautiful time together for those few hours once a week. No matter what has happened in our individual lives before that day, we set aside all those things for the purpose of worshiping together.

Here, in these hours, it doesn't matter what our age, race, or socioeconomic status is; we are all one as a family. My church family wants for me the same things that my birth family wants for me. We are concerned and care about the health and well-being of each member of the church.

I love going to church and being of service to help the church thrive. I love welcoming each member and visitors who come, knowing that in the next hour we will be celebrating our coming together for one purpose, which is to worship together.

Travel Adventures

I'm standing on a corner in a large city, and I hear several different languages being spoken. As I cross the street, I see people of all ages and various nationalities.

Hoping I'm standing in the right line for the downtown bus, I ask a man if this is the correct spot. Although the city I'm visiting is an English-speaking country, I don't understand a single word the man has spoken.

Not knowing anything but "good morning" and "goodbye" in the language spoken in this foreign city, I approach a woman to ask her for directions to a popular tourist spot. I say "Excuse me," and then point as I'm saying the name of the building. I was hoping that by pointing, she might understand that I needed help in finding the spot, but she looked at me like I was from Mars.

While sitting behind the driver of a cart that was taking me to a tourist spot, the driver wanted to know my opinion of the U.S. president and if this president was good for the country.

A cab driver asks me, after finding out what country I'm from, if where I live is close to where his sister lives. He asks me if the distance is about 30 miles from where I live. I tell him no; it would take almost a day to drive from my city to where his sister lives.

The man behind the hotel check-in stops for a moment before handing me my key to the door and goes to speak with another person behind the desk. When he comes back, he tells me that they are going to upgrade my room to a suite. The room was larger than my one-bedroom apartment.

A van comes to pick me up at the hotel to take me to the location where I am to board a bus for the sightseeing tour. I'm the only one in the van, and the two men in the front seat start talking and laughing with one another in their language. Immediately, the theme song from *The Godfather* starts playing in my head. I think I'm about to get whacked.

There is nothing more exciting to me than traveling alone to a different city. Having to depend on the kindness of strangers and my intuition is what keeps me traveling to new places. And... it's not just the physical sights that are great to see; but the conversations with the strangers I meet that make the trips so rewarding.

Friendships

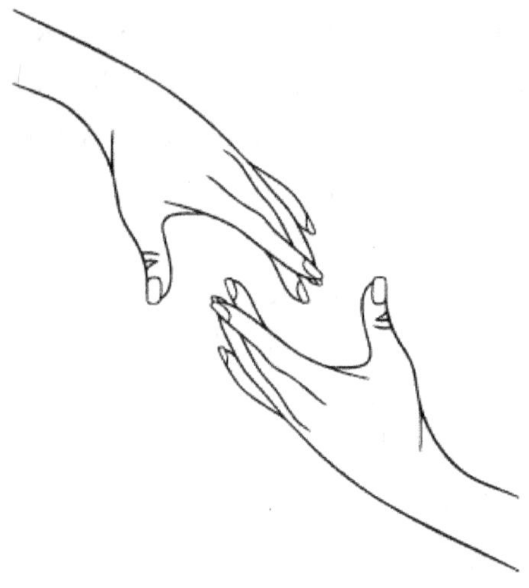

Growing up, I had several friends I walked to school with or had classes with. We were similar in personalities, and it was fun to share those times with someone who wasn't family. I didn't realize how important it is to have a good friend until I went to college. It was the first time I was living away from home and sharing a dorm room with a stranger. There was the happiness of not living at home, but also the anxiety of knowing I had to make decisions now that would affect my future. Since family and friends have ideas about what you should be doing with your life and what direction it should take, I had to make it clear to myself what I wanted in life.

When I started working, it became very important for me to start thinking about which of the people I was calling my friends were actually good influences in my life. Some were just interested in partying every weekend and just getting by during the work week. There wasn't much thought about what we saw in our future or if any of us had a good plan or ambition to do more with our lives.

Then it happened—the time when it really hit home on looking at who I thought was a good friend. I called a friend one night to say I thought I needed to go back into therapy. We had been friends for several years; I even went to visit her when she moved out of town with her husband, but this call ended the relationship. Expecting her to be sympathetic and ask me what was wrong, she told me that a favorite television show was coming on and she wanted to watch it. I said okay, could I call her when the show was over? She said no; she would call me tomorrow. She never called. The next day I thought about all the times I had been there for her, but now I needed her and she wasn't available. We never talked again.

There is a Bible verse that talks about being a good friend, John 15:13. When I know that a friend is in need, I set aside my life, whatever I'm doing, to be there for them.

Most of the studies I've read about what elderly people regret the most about their lives is that they did not spend much time nurturing their relationships with family and friends. When my apartment building caught fire and residents were not allowed back into the building, several friends provided shelter for me until I could get a new apartment weeks later.
I need friends!

Bridges

I remember when I was younger, visiting my great-grandmother in Virginia, and we went to see another relative there who lived across a stream. In order to get to his house, we had to cross an old rope bridge with wooden planks. Since the bridge was old, several of the planks were missing, and you could see the stream flowing below. I think we were at least 12 feet above the stream, and I was afraid to cross it.

A bridge connects two things. Bridges help us move quicker and easier from one side to the other. Bridges have been around since the beginning of time, and their construction and design change frequently now because of modern materials. Thinking of the rope bridge I crossed as a young child, I start wondering about the "bridges" I've used in my life so far. What relationships, jobs, and education did I need to help me get from one side to the other? Would I trust using that old rope bridge now? The bridges I use today, what do I trust about them? How solid and trustworthy are they that I feel safe using them? I've had relationships, jobs, and even taken some additional schooling in order to cross over into a new adventure, new jobs, and even new apartments, but sometimes the support was not there.

There is a movie titled *Murder by Death*, in which one of the stars, Peter Sellers, and his son are about to drive across a rickety bridge. Peter Sellers gets out of the car and tells his son to drive across to see if the bridge is safe. The son successfully drives the car very carefully across the bridge. After doing so, Peter Sellers tells his son to now drive back across the bridge and pick him up.

How do I test the bridges in my future? Do I need to see how others have crossed over, or do I just trust my instinct and cautiously move across?

The Moon

I believe the reason why I love looking at the moon so much is that it was the first celestial body I saw. I actually thought I could just walk far enough and I would be on the moon. I will never forget that evening when this thought came to me. My family lived at the bottom of a dead-end street, and one night on our way somewhere, when the family's car crested the hill, there it was—the moon. It was so large, so close to the horizon, that I was in awe. How could it be possible for humans to be so close to this natural body in the sky? This was before the United States landed on the moon in 1969. I remember that day also. The whole family was sitting in the living room watching the TV screen when Neil Armstrong exited the spacecraft and walked on the moon.

The reason I'm a big fan of science fiction stories is that I grew up watching television shows such as *Twilight Zone, Star Trek,* and *Lost in Space*. I wanted to be one of the astronauts living on the spaceship in *Star Trek*. I was fascinated with space travel then, and I still am. I purchased a telescope several years ago just so I could look at the craters on the moon.

There is a television series called *Ancient Aliens*, and in one of the episodes, they talked about how the moon might be hollow. The show also said that aliens might have a base station on the far side of the moon because we will never be able to see that side of the moon unless we go there. While this remains to be proven— whether or not the moon is hollow or occupied by aliens—I'm still in awe that I can see the surface of the moon through my telescope.

What's the bigger picture for me in thinking about the moon? There's a natural body that circles the Earth and reflects the light from the sun. The moon is constantly there, every day and night, even though on certain days of

the month, such as the new moon, we can't
see it.

37

So... who else orbits me and provides me
light, day and night?

Fork in the Road

I remember thinking as a child that I couldn't wait to become an adult. Adults had all the answers, so decision-making would be easier. Every day there is a fork in the road. Every day we make what can seem like minor decisions—decisions that can have dramatic effects on our future. Which bus to take, drive the freeway or the back roads, whether to go to the office today even though I don't feel well, etc. Usually I let my intuition tell me which road to take, and when I do so, most times I find myself running into someone I haven't seen in years. Some of the decisions we encounter on the fork in the road are based on what we see in our future or which way the economy is heading.

I'll never forget how early in my working life, I had the chance to take a shorthand class at the large corporation where I was working. I thought taking this class might help me move out of the typing pool and I could become a secretary. However, I had a sense that using shorthand was not a skill that was going to be around much longer. I believed that the technology would find another way to improve how bosses gave dictation of their correspondence.

I purchased a car one year because I had to use two buses to get to my job. During the winter months, waiting for two buses was not a pleasant experience. I hated owning a car, and several months later, I ended up being laid off and had to get rid of the car because I couldn't afford to pay the car loan. When I was looking for future employment after that job, I made sure that the location of the company I was considering working for would not require me to use two buses to get there. I have never owned a car since.

My favorite fork in the road is the one I took to take an art history class at the Carnegie Museum of Art. Thirty years prior to taking the class, I was in my aunt's kitchen telling her that when I retired, I wanted to become a docent at the museum. I didn't even know what the word docent meant and had to look it up. I was given this word, docent! It came out of my mouth without realizing what I was saying. In January of 2019, I was looking through the Carnegie Museum of Art's website for a class to take since I was retired and had previously taken drawing lessons there. In the description for the art history class, it said that this class was a prerequisite for becoming a docent. I was shocked. Here was that word again that I spoke to my aunt over thirty years ago. The class was starting in two weeks, and I had to make the decision of

whether to sign up or look for something else
to do. Taking the class was the perfect road
for me. Becoming a docent is my raison d'être,
the most important role of service in my life.
Sharing art with visitors from all over the
world brings me much joy, and it was the
correct road I chose.

One World Trade Center

Whenever I travel to New York City, I try to make a stop at One World Observatory. It's my way of supporting the idea that evil does not win. I remember September 11, 2001. I was working in one of the tallest buildings in downtown Pittsburgh, and the building management told all offices to vacate because they were not sure if there were more planes in the air that might target taller buildings in other cities. Like many others, I was in shock watching the video at home of how quickly the two towers fell. I have a photo of me sitting in the Windows on the World restaurant that was on the 107th floor of the North Tower. How was it possible that this building would go down so quickly?

In life, there are moments when I think this building, this relationship, this job is rock solid and nothing will take it down. But in reality, there are things, relationships, and even ideas that fall apart. Some things fall in an instant and others through a slow, gradual collapse.

I think about what the building means to me. It's a visible representation of what resurrection is about. Resurrection is restoration, giving strength back to that which was weak, and life being brought back from death. I've been there. So depressed I considered suicide. But God restored me, bringing me back from the thought that death was better than life. Now I stand tall, like the One World Trade Center. I know the feeling of collapse, being brought down. And now I know the joy of resurrection.

Family

How do I define the word "family"? First, it's your birth parents and your common ancestors. Second, there are those like myself who weren't raised by our birth family; hence, family is a group of people living together as a unit. Third, there are families made up of a group of people with a common idea or related things. I currently have three families: my birth family, my church family, and the group of docents I volunteer with at the museum.

I consider myself rich for having such loving family members. I can't change who is part of my birth family, but the other families I have

are just as important to me. Each family
wants what is best for me and wants me to
continue to grow and be happy. Each family is
composed of people of different ages and
races, and I need all of these relationships to
help me become who I am. I can depend on
my family members when I am in need. I pray
for them and enjoy time spent in their
company.

We can't exist without a family. It's in family
relationships that we learn about love and
forgiveness. It's my family relationships that
invite me to continue to be the best person I
can be.